This Wandering State:

Poems from Alta

Volume I: San Francisco *edited by Kim Shuck*

This Wandering State: Poems from Alta Volume I: San Francisco

Copyright © 2022 CALIBA
ISBN 979-8-9851707-0-2

All rights reserved by the individual authors and artists, except for fair use in reviews
and/or scholarly considerations.

Cover and Title Page Image © Megan Wilson
Layout Design © Douglas A. Salin
Introduction © Kim Shuck
Editor © Kim Shuck

Early Summer, Pandemic Year by Kathleen McClung previously published in <u>Three Soul-Makers: Poems That Bring Us Together</u>
Wapshott Press, 2021

Electric System, by Sunnylyn Thibodeaux first appeared in <u>The World Exactly</u>/Cuneiform Press/2020

Elegy For The Castro Funeral Home by James Siegel first appeared in <u>The God of San Francisco</u> by Sibling Rivalry Press

I'm a Poverty Skola by Kimo Umu and
Making Business Proposals with Ancestral Lands
by Phillip Standing Bear first appeared in <u>pooramagazine.org</u>

Save Me San Francisco by Christine No first appeared in
<u>Whatever Love Means</u> by Barrelhouse 2021

https://caliballiance.org

This work was mostly created on the unceded lands of the Ramaytush people. We honor and respect their ongoing relationship and stewardship of this place.

Foreword

San Francisco has been fugitive for a while now. Everyone who comes here sees part of what they left somewhere else. It's what the 'west' has generally been used for: some imaginary blank slate. It's not blank and never was, but it's been used for that so definitions are always serving suggestions and not always useful. Those of us born here, resident in our formative years, or even of First Peoples, will see something else. I haven't figured out how to midwife those understandings and I may never manage that leap. Sitting at my kitchen table, staring at San Bruno Mountain in the fog, cat at the front door singing street cat poems, that's what San Francisco is for me at this very moment. When the fog burns off things will be different. Anthologies are as tricky as definitions. Is this a complete anthology of San Francisco poetry? No. There are no complete anthologies. I served San Francisco as her 7th Poet Laureate. I was born and grew up here. I love the place and the poetry. There is much in the way of poetry. This is some of it.

K. Shuck
2nd Late Summer of the Pandemic
in the Fog

Table of Contents

	Kathleen McClung	11
Early Summer, Pandemic Year		
Sounds of the City 2	**Jennifer Barone**	13
Eating leftovers on the 31	**Mason J**	14
Three Memories	**Adrian Arias**	15
We Be Guardians	**Kitty Costello**	17
Colonized American Daughters	**E.K. Keith**	19
top of fort point	**Lisbit Bailey**	20
Born to Local Precincts	**Tongo Eisen-Martin**	21
	Tehmina Khan	23
Maya Angelou At City College of San Francisco		
Electric System	**Sunnylyn Thibodeaux**	25
Wistful on the Picket Line	**Randy James**	26
Arrival As We	**Lauren Ito**	27
Hand	**Anna Lisa Escobedo**	28
We Are All Part of One Another	**Nancy Hom**	29
Stage IIa	**Preeti Vangani**	31
A Good Rain	**Clara Hsu**	33
Wild and Lost in the City	**Michael Warr**	34
Broken Sonnet For San Francisco	**Dean Rader**	35
San Francisco Fountain	**Ruth Asawa**	36
	James Siegel	37
Elegy For The Castro Funeral Home		
The Tusks	**Karthik Sethuraman**	39
Kiss	**Adrian Arias**	40
Jaws	**MK Chavez**	41

42 **Florencia Milito**   Lullaby
43 **Florencia Milito**   Canción De Cuna
44 **Kim Shuck**   Raven Bag
45 **K.R. Morrison**   Bone Mother
46 **Kimo Umu**   Im a Poverty skola
47 **Norm Mattox**   notes to my self
49 **Christine No**   Save Me San Francisco
51 **Jack Hirschman**   In Memoriam George Guess
53 **devorah major**   san francisco beach blues
55 **Lourdes Figueroa**   Raw
58 **Phillip Standing Bear**
   Making Business Proposals with Ancestral Lands
59 **Mahnaz Badihian**   For Fay (Fataneh)
61 **Tiny/ PovertySkola**
   The Violent Act of Looking Away
63 **Paul Corman-Roberts**
   The Longest 12 Seconds
65 **Charlie Getter**   Spanish boats
68 **Susan Kitazawa**   School Nurse
73 **William Lautner**   We ARE Different
75 **Greg Pond**   the fillmore or less
77 **Kim Shuck**   San Francisco

80 **Contributors**

This Wandering State:

Poems from Alta

San Francisco

edited by Kim Shuck

Dedication

There are songs that attempted genocide has stolen for all time. Even so, I would like to thank the poets who created them. I may not know you individually, but we love some of the same things, and that has to be a connection.

My thanks also to Calvin Crosby and Ann Seaton for time spent and vast patience. Morgan and Ed for game therapy. Paul for being part of the team no matter what the weather is: storm, wildfire or protest.

Doug, there really will never be enough words.

Finally, my thanks to this place.

Kathleen McClung
Early Summer, Pandemic Year

At twilight, a bridge not far from here
        begins humming.
Wind rattles panes, the soot decades old,
and we nod: familiar percussion at room's edge.
Beyond, a virus skates a rink the size of Venus.
So many puzzles: why Nancy fell from her bike.
Whose hunger pushed our cart aisles away.
Where in the tall grass that emerald earring sleeps.
I want to return, doze midafternoon, barefoot,
our faces, yours and mine, open completely,
the egrets and turtles of Stow Lake breathing, alert.
May we wake to a cure for the sickness
and beside my cheek, a small green stone.

Beside my cheek, a small green stone,
we wake to a cure for the sickness,
the egrets and turtles of Stow Lake, breathing, alert.
Our faces, yours and mine, open completely.
We have returned, dozed midafternoon, barefoot
in the tall grass. That emerald earring slept.
A hunger pushed our hearts. Miles away,
so many puzzles! Why Nancy fell from her bike

beyond. A virus once skated a rink the size of Venus.
We nod. Familiar percussion at room's edge:
wind rattles panes, the soot decades old, and
at twilight, a bridge not far from here
        begins humming.

Jennifer Barone
Sounds of the City 2

when the fog arrived unannounced
San Francisco complained

she says, ships no longer need it
given new technologies

perhaps we missed
the echo of our longing cry
into the abyss

there is a silence
at the edge of the world
that can break your heart

Mason J

Eating leftovers on the 31 Balboa

I promise to *five-finger discount fork clanking in your
    purse* you
If your heart can palpitate *parka pockets stuffed full
    with spring roll affections,* me right back.
We'll come together mouth to scorching tongue
Wrapped in gooey Tony's Pizza drool
My meat mind a Russian piroshki,
your body an overstuffed La Corneta burrito.

We'll eat until it hurts
Feeding seagulls leftover love at Ocean Beach
Tossing crows carne asada carrion in McLaren Park
The heavens twist Cioppino into Eggplant Parmesan.
And our crunchy sunset romance of
    Casa Sanchez chips n salsa
Slides from pinky nail moon
    to an elbow-shaped constellation.

I guess what I am trying to say is…
I adore you most when you're squeezing my chest
In mouthfuls of Divisadero Cheesesteaks.
Rolled up like Maruya futomaki on Fillmore
Holding tighter than Thanh Tam II to-go boxes.

Adrian Arias

January 2021, in pandemic.
Three Memories

one

I cut my nails and I remember my mother.
She told me
"Adrián, think carefully
where you are going to leave or throw your nails,
because where they stay you will collect them
        one by one,
after you have died."

Today I left my nails in the forest.
Next time it will be in front of the sea,
and then I will leave some at the entrance of your house.

two

At night, when I look at the sky,
I remember my grandmother pointing to a star and
        saying to me
"Look Adrián, in that one there is a child like you,
but he is already a grandfather and has a granddaughter
        by his side,

and together they are looking at the sky, they are looking
>   over here,
where you and I are now".

I know I asked her many questions,
but what I remember the most
is the hug she gave me.

three

Today I dreamed of the beach of my childhood
and I remembered my aunts in the kitchen
talking fondly with a fish and telling me
"Don't be scared Adrián, we are not crazy but
it is important to talk to each thing that you are
>   going to eat,
it is important to caress the vegetables and
>   kiss the fruits "

I'm kissing my tomatoes, caressing my lettuce
and conversing kindly with my olive oil,
this will be a happy salad.

Kitty Costello
We Be Guardians

Casting a spell now
in the face of hatred's bare teeth,
bringing forward what is best
in each and all, now
in our hour of need,
the beast breath upon us.

Sacred Ones of all times past,
stay near. Banish
the loss of heart we can't afford.
Breathe valiance through each live
body standing, yielding and strong.
I pray you may forgive us,
you who are to come.

Feel the mesh now
of the web being sewn
and unweave it as fast as you can
with fierce, unflinching love.
Remember what it feels like
when truth is being told.

Stand with ease in what is good.
There are so many right notes to sing.
The chorus is swearing
on all that has brought us
to the edge of this battlefield,
each flesh body facing fire.

Do not fret over grave
regrettables untold.
The whole deck is in play at once.
Grab a last look or a last book
on the way out the door,
yesterday collapsing,
divine dictation persisting.
Laughter is portable.
Check your emergency kit.

May our nerve-flow travel
at the pace of peace.
What does it mean to have a spine
or to dive in
to these salt pools of grief?

Attend each tolling bell.
Bless it all.
All days are holy.
All sacred in water,
on earth,
in dreams.

We be guardians.

E.K. Keith
Colonized American Daughters

English has left me speechless
in at least three Other languages

My mother tongue
ate up all the words
that might have been mine

If you can't say it
you can't think it
and you can't do it

What's left   all that's left
a few family keepsakes
some quaint old trinkets
a recipe or two
self-loathing
a desire to fit in

This is how Wisdom gets lost
and never comes home

Lisbit Bailey
top of fort point

for the first time I climbed
three flights of stairs to the top of fort point
I climbed and walked, looked and thought
about the story in these old bricks

post-gold rush, pre-civil war
between bay and ocean
rescue equipment below
the bridge to save the unsaved

weakness bound with loss
depression, desire for more
better, different, another lot in life
the commonplace plague

unguarded, I keep looking for a way
to climb to new vantage points to see
for the first time again because
where joy visits, I want to linger

Tongo Eisen-Martin
Born to Local Precincts

I like this side of the city
    the side that Queen mothers watch over

tutoring the commune meetings
bringing prosperity to the revolution

holy, holy handshakes/the drums you love while kneeling
                      or unintelligible chariot-talk

    Good suggestions on all side of my friend's passing

Lower the correct casket this time

Sneak the same eyes into your master's stomach
    Your dangerous imagination running with a factory rat
    sardine tin rex
    revolution colors on the soles
    from walking with a knife over astronomy books
                  in the new South living room

We got married in secret at the Black Power conference
Wearing modest underground clothes
Made in Black San Francisco

I don't think I'm being followed, momma
maybe studied a little

maybe I can sketch you, Lord

or at least the veins of red in my eyes

Tehmina Khan
Maya Angelou
At City College of San Francisco

Poetry Month, 2019
We are Poets for the People
gathered tight
in a City College classroom
in the presence of Maya Angelou
resurrected by memory and love.
We rise
to speak her words
in Tagalog
Portuguese
Urdu
Spanish
French
Chinese
We rise in Hawaiian
in Tigrinya
in Arabic
in Japanese
With drum beat
and guitar strums,
we speak her words,

witness four hundred years
of resistance,
and emerge in silver sequins
like our ancestor the fish,
rising out of the ocean
to start life anew.
Poets for the People,
we seek that maternal
heartbeat of the earth,
holding us close,
then lifting us up.
In these new nights of terror,
what choice do we have?
Poets must do what poets do.
We rise.
Yes, they want to see us broken.
They always have.
They want to shut down poetry.
But we are Poets for the People,
a black ocean
swelling with truth.
And Maya Angelou
in the Great Beyond?
We have her poem.
And we rise.

Sunnylyn Thibodeaux
Electric System

We've got King tides
and Alice Coltrane sweeping
up the mood. It's Christmas Eve
and Japantown is overrun with littered
umbrellas and nitro puffs. Safeway smeared
with footprints and a Salvation
Army Santa playing a recorder
with his little red collection bucket. An emergency
landing at SFO. Rain is still pouring
through a hole in the roof. 94-year-old
landlord stopped in yesterday to say hello. Shit
came out when he saw the gape. Get an estimate
Rent hasn't been cashed making the account
seem inflated for delight. Santa Tracker
is running despite the government's
shutdown over a lack of empathy and an orange
man's temper tantrum. The spirit of giving
doesn't live in everyone. It isn't supposed to
Our shoulders are strong, and we will
continue to carry joy into the night
across borders of religion and race
because that one wish is the persistent hope
that we make it to know love in its
boundless array of faith. That we make it
to know love

                    The World Exactly/Cuneiform Press/2020

Randy James
Wistful on the Picket Line

Of the men who gripped silence to the grave:

> How many kissed their mirrors, lost
> their breath & bent for curled biceps big
> enough to lie in? How many brush-by's
> & electric glances recalled in self-play
> to assuage the ache? How many dreams
> in 50's anything? Horned rims, Cadillacs and
> cool creams, ducktails and cigarette
> machines? Drive-ins where quarter
> & running backs nibble kernel backseat?
> What about floats & their cherries?
> How many loved in substitution? Joined twin
> beds? Wife & children, mistresses – serial
> understudies? How many gym locker room
> silhouettes? Promise rings in bunk beds?
> "Show me yours, show you mine" home
> alone? What about moons in uncle's
> bedroom? Glances back in Tomorrowland?
> How many shoeless footsies in school
> libraries? Playful ass grabs in Physical
> Science? How many cap-covered eyes down
> alleyways? "Never again" entering
> the bathhouse? How many Marthas
> at the door?

Lauren Ito
Arrival As We

Thousands of women hum in my blood
Forced to play god
Cradled their knives with a gentle hand
Lifted gazes to the horizon
And summoned air
Tucked it into laugh lines
A teacup
A birthmark
A prayer
For generations yet to unfurl
Knowing breath is never promised
Always
Especially these days
Always.
Always.
Remember this
Inhaling sunrise and birdsong

We never arrive alone.

Anna Lisa Escobedo
Hand

Nancy Hom
We Are All Part of One Another
Tribute to Yuri Kochiyama, 4-30-17

To be part of one another is to know
That when you breathe I heave with you
And when you sigh I cry beside you.
We are breath and water, each of us
Passing from one vessel to another
In the mandala of life.

Knowing this, we would delve into
The deepest part of ourselves
To see the brilliance inside others.
We would be more careful with words
And protest deeds that hurt and harm.
We would guard the earth
As if it were our hallowed home.

Knowing we are not separate
We fight for freedom and justice
With fierce rage cupped in compassion.
For we cannot be free if one of us is not.
We cannot reap riches if one of us has none.
We cannot fully love if one of us is hated.

Fight for prisoners wrongly jailed.
Protect the rights of women raped.
Free all immigrants detained by ICE.
Stand with Muslims against the ban.
Rebuild black churches burned by hate.

Fight for sacred land and clean water.
Preserve mountains, forests, and streams.
Protest greedy politicians' plunder.
Cry for bears shot in their sleep.
Control the climate before it's too late.

Beyond her life, Yuri's words live on
In every continent, every country, every town.
"We are all part of one another."
Rise up and fight as one.

Preeti Vangani
Stage IIa

The famous doctor, who is highly skilled
in optimism says, mastectomy
is just not needed for my mother. He looks
at her breasts, cups his hands
in prayer to mean: these are god's gifts.
Rain falls like god
is moved and something the size
of a glass marble moves
inside my mother. Only this time
it is not as simple as her sadness.
On their way out, my dad gathers
her chest scans, her hand, his courage
and says, *We are not worried at all,*
doctor sahab, about vanity, remove it
if needed. God is so pleased, the city
gets its full rain within five days.
Everywhere is life, perhaps too much
life except mummy spits blood
into kerchiefs with the same grace
as kissing prayers into our foreheads
and by winter dad and I must acclimatize

to live inside the nip of *If-only* sentences.
Was the doctor's decision a medical one
or a man's on what a woman must have
to look like a woman? We cry with the other
not looking. And when he tells this story,
my dad, about what he didn't know
would become the last evening he stood
in water with her, he leads
with the bright color of the umbrella
they left behind in the examination room.

Clara Hsu
A Good Rain
from *"Chinatown Snapshots"*

Tall boy Hang Ah dissolves
into a funhouse mirror
but Willy Woo Woo
has no playmates today
One white umbrella
bounces down the slope
My little jellyfish
the water is running
        road workers
        old lurkers
they go underground
        all because
there's a good rain
pouring from the infinity pot
cold simmer   white tea
red lanterns   on a tightrope
ping pang ping-pong
The grass is fake but the pigeons are real
One's for the running feet and one's my love
Dennis' sculptures and Antonio's art
coffee, weed and exercise
the story goes
But who's there to hear it?

Michael Warr
Wild and Lost in the City
(Gough and Eddy, San Francisco, CA / 2015)

Manicured fingers of Jackson Square Park
soothe the paws of a lonesome cougar
stalking survival down wild streets.

In the moon-lit backdrop breaking through
a cloud-pierced canopy City Hall's gilded dome
hovers-a glowing like a spaced-out starship.

Surveilling streetlamps capture
the big cat's nocturnal pacing, faux sunlight
glistening against its golden coat.

It strides by dead mountains we sleep in
safely behind white stone and windowpanes
sensing the tracks of its exiled ancestors.

The Fillmore waits.

Dean Rader
Broken Sonnet For San Francisco

The birds have zipped   up their suits of feathers
and flown   again   from there to   here.
Their bones tiny sticks of smoke.   The air /

The air. And now the street.   And yet   St. Francis
moves among the bags / the boxes
of women
           and men unfolding on the
sidewalk the way a heart splits

into a basket   of bread. There are   no
symbols for hunger in Medieval paintings.
Surely the lord / comes to the weak and
                              famished / to the lost

and forgotten. Surely,   a lord   comes. In the   absence
of   everything but the morning light /
the saint walks along Market street.   No one   except

the ghosts rise
           to follow.

photo ©2021 Douglas A. Salin

Ruth Asawa
San Francisco Fountain, 1970-1973

Artwork © 2021 Ruth Asawa Lanier, Inc.

James Siegel
Elegy For The Castro Funeral Home

One hundred years and you are gone.
Death is not the business it once was.
Monument to loss—your crumbling
façade a reminder of days we would rather
forget.   But forgetting
is just more dying.

  So who will remember you
when the bulldozer and the wrecking
ball levels your walls, clears the way
for more overpriced homes?

When new bones rise from your foundation
and jackhammers turn concrete to dust
will anyone listen for benedictions
haunting the dusty air?
Will anyone pry loose a century of eulogies
trapped in the earth? And will they pour forth
from the pavement cracks like steam—
a pale ghost—ascending the sky?

From your ashes a tower of condos
for the living—East Coast dreamers seeking
a California mythology, too young to know
the power of death or a quilt of names a mile long.

Will they know where they sleep at night?
And will they wake in dark hours to the sweet
perfume of gardenias, lilies? Wake to the burning
of vigil candles, the honey scent of soft wax,
smoke and ember from dying flames?

And when they gut your front parlor
for a coffee shop or sidewalk café,
will anyone remember the dead in repose?
Will anyone sip a morning brew and witness
phantom pallbearers, another casket carried
out your front door? Day after day,
week after week—how did you keep up
with death's punctual schedule?
As many as three funerals a day
in that decade of decimation.

Will anyone remember you
as the only mortuary in San Francisco
to open its doors to the victims of AIDS?
In those days even the dead were turned away.
But you dressed them in suits and ties,
washed and combed their hair, powdered
the skin to hide the scars and sores,
made them into handsome young men again.

So will we remember or will we build
and build again? Turning earth over and
over until history is another buried thing.

Karthik Sethuraman
The Tusks

In the backroom
beneath a faded tablecloth
the remains of beasts
my ancestors killed
or paid for bartered
or bought I never lifted
the shroud the outlines
were enough the outlines
and the carving of our god
in the mud his animal head
above the doorway
descending the morning
I never lifted the dust
and what I wasn't afraid
to ask why should we cover
our shame in the shadow
the rifle glinting the holiness
and always where to shoot
the thing so that its face
might still resemble
the face of our god.

Adrian Arias
Kiss

MK Chavez
Jaws

The tension goes on for eighty-one minutes
before we actually see the creature.

Is it vagina dentata or is it Maybelline?

Consider fine china.
A spiked venetian chastity belt.

Florencia Milito
Lullaby

> eyes & trees
> eyes & trees
> & maybe a bee
>
> I know words will not
> stop the armies
>
> or the tortures
>
> and these days I think
> of little besides
>
> Still I draw
> imaginary trees
> eyes & trees
> eyes & trees
> & even a bee

Florencia Milito
Canción de cuna

ojos y árboles
ojos y árboles
y quizás una abeja

Sé que las palabras
no detendrán
ni a los ejércitos

ni a las torturas

y estos días pienso
en poca otra cosa

Pero aún dibujo
árboles imaginarios
árboles y ojos
árboles y ojos
y quizás una abeja

Kim Shuck
Raven Bag

K.R. Morrison
Bone Mother

at a crossroads, She meets you in shadows
        Dark Moon Mother, together
you walk through dead battles, old scars
scattered in nightlands cold
        like bones at your feet, like bones
holding stories, eras old
        you're ready to shed, bones
holding magick, new phases await
        so next to Her, you shed baby moonskin

in Her shadowlands, you hear ancestors
        hymning, behind them Bone Mother
the Night Queen of the Crossroads sings

    fear not those old soul tangles, leave the
        past at Mother Earth's feet
    I have you witch daughter, shed that little
        girl free
    let your inner goddess bloom, give all that
        death to me

Kimo Umu
Im a Poverty skola
excerpt from poormagazine.org

Yo Im a poverty SKola, with a chip on sholda. Still fighting the system keepin it goin like soulja. When times get rough and tough, N im like i had enough, I pick myself up to break outta these cuffs. Liberating my conscious, as yall look in astonishment. Racking knockouts like my name is jack johnson. Freedom from this system, breaking down the parliament

Norm Mattox
notes to my self

itsa good thing
im writing poetry
to express my outrage.
that and meditation,
saves me from immolating
self regularly
recomposing my self from ashes
stay home,
breathe one breath at a time,
appreciate simple blessings
itsa good thing
im staying 'remote' from
the community protests
i don't want to threaten
my self, being co-opted
by chaotic rage.
emotional boundaries overrun
by stampede i am more concerned
by the mob within
death is not incidental to protest.
i have a difficult time

deciding what to live for
used to be
life was lived for
motherless dawtas
making plans
life interrupted
with reasons to die
definitely not safe while
covertly targeted
for my profile
i make amends
with the reaper
live life 40 minutes
in fronna me…
ima do my best to stay safe
in my melanin skin
that's the long fight

ancestors remind me
the ongoing struggle is life,
gonna meditate harder
write peace i can share

Christine No
Save Me San Francisco

Today is Monday and
I was born two days ago.

I want to apologize but
What for?

This strange betrayal
This lightness of being: my wet towel heart wrung
over a city

I thought would save me. *April showers!*

in San Francisco
The weight of you lingers.

My dry heart hung
I ghost up & down sidewalks

feather light sternum: empty birdcage
the bottoms of my feet, indoor palms pale white
and skyward—

I am a prayer, perhaps.

Hovering supine, the magician's assistant, Sputnik
weaving streets and alleys—hills and
      secret stairwells
North and South of Market St.

I'm told this place can make a cat of a girl,
      rewind time
a *little bit;* that strange things still exist,
      secrets tucked

Between tourists & tech workers
Pocket magnetized, abuzz-ing sunshine

& sidewalk pawing grace
Softer landings, please—

I was told this place would change a girl—

Jack Hirschman
In Memoriam George Guess
August 7, 2020

On your birthday,
George Guess,
a few days after
you passed away,

how can a giant
Sequoia not be
beginning to grow
in the woods

where you will
be buried? You,
who've the same
name as that

creator of the
syllabary of the
Cherokee people,
as you've given

brilliant voice to
the people of
Yorkshire with
your paintings.

Grow tall in death,
George Guess,
with your always
deep wit and

humor of what
is wisdom's
highest, most
glorious sky.

devorah major
san francisco beach blues

i hear its sough and sigh as it washes refuse
        onto the shore
more frequently than the shells I used to capture

more frequently than the smooth stones

i used to pick up and finger
before warming them in my palms
and almost always dropping each stone
back to the shore's damp edge

i want its
ancient ocean scent to sidle into my nostrils
moist kelp vines beginning to dry, to rot

gull emptied tiny crab carcasses

i thirst for the salt that envelops the air

fills my mouth
lingers on the edges of my lashes
i yearn for the beach spume-rich and noisy

before its sand was turned matte black

& steel gray, hiding

its soft tan skin beneath smelted oil
its foam skirts full of trash

dying fish and marooned whales
we need to return it again to its wealth
to steer our sturdy ships to the garbage patch

hovering between hawaii and california

awash from crest to trough with plastic scum

and fill the vessels' holds with our putrid waste

return it to its source
to help the ocean again croon her song of the living
a hymn for her children growing in deep sea forests
nourished on the edges of underwater mountains

bred in the steam of her submerged volcanos

Lourdes Figueroa
Raw

    & I could see

    the syllables

    of our bodies

    become the embers

    of the firewood

    burning out

    soft cold night

    in the middle

    of the woods

    pine

    cedar

    woods

    & I don't

    recall our campsite

    but there you were,

    there I was

    your mouth

    holding a story

     older than

the makeup
around your eyes
stars on your
cheeks
reflecting
firewood light
& like all the poets
I wanted to give
this poem to you
raw
but I realized
raw is relative
it could mean
medium rare
to some
well done to
others
so I decided
the most raw
would be
if you pulled
the poem out
from a chest
still breathing

then the poem
as it is pulled out
will have fog breath
outside the body
will be warm
for many full
minutes
even in my palm
it will be warm as
I pass it on
warm and raw
still beating
because it still
thinks
it is alive
just in the same
way
we offered
sacrifices
when we
knew
the goddxxs
that made us

Phillip Standing Bear
Making Business Proposals with Ancestral Lands-
excerpt from poormagazine.org

"Paha Sapa, The heart of everything that is" at least that is what my people, the Lakota Sioux Nation, say about our homeland. The dark black rolling hills filled with the smell of pure oxygen thanks to the pine trees, sticky with sweet smelling sap made by my peoples as a syrup source, small clear creeks filled with minnows. Hot and green during the summer and cold and snowy during the winter. The tall majestic pines are a testament to the Earths' fertile, dark pungent soil, which I think of when thinking of the struggle of Oak Flats. The Lakota creeks were clean enough to drink from, the sky always blue and clear, even when a storm rolled through, the Paha Sapa changed any fearsome storm to a calming downpour with the smells of the pines only amplified with the rain. Any snowstorm was well welcomed with the thought of being surrounded by "Christmas Trees" as children. Paha Sapa, like any land as gracious as that, would be considered sacred lands, but as we say here at Deecolonize Academy, nothing left is sacred.

Mahnaz Badihian
For Fay (Fataneh)

The day I was riding on the Ferry from
       San Francisco
I saw someone was walking on the surface
of the Ocean who was dead years ago,
and the ocean we love with its endless beauty
had a chest filled with drama, screaming
with the echoing voices of the dead,
and the wounds of unfortunate sailors
with the melody of the corps of migrating birds.

While each new wave was swallowing the
       previous wave
the ocean had a gift for forgotten dead
The gift of blood on its shores.
The gift of the lifeless body of Ilan Kordies
with a piece of their mother's dress in their fist
The gift of lost pair of shoes arriving with
each wave from unknown rivers and oceans

 I was sitting in the Ferry early morning
I felt burned the ocean,s heart from
black oil dripping on its blue chest from tankers
from the black boxes drowned with
the destiny of countless lovers.

Sitting in the Ferry in that foggy morning
towards San Quentin
where the body of Fay was found years ago.
From the window, I looked at grayish,
      restless water
and saw that Fay's eyes repeating itself
in thousands in a circular motion
on the chest of the Pacific ocean.
Her long hair has covered
the surface of the cold water
trying to be a nest for the lost birds

I stretch my hands to grab her
from the threshold of death
but she was hand in hand, disappearing
with hundreds of people who lost their
      last breath
in the Pacific ocean!
I lost a friend and her image in the same water.

Tiny/ PovertySkola
The Violent Act of Looking Away
Poem/Palabraz
From the MamaLogues theatre series -Sterile

Why did u leave me? Why did u leave and go
away - taking my heart and throwing it goddam
muthfukinwhor street- u are a whore- anyway,slept
with bush-iknowit i saw it-
why did u leave and go away?

Her hair was long strands sailing in the night air
with no people that wonder or care about her and
only people who want her out of sight

My mama-used to say- "one day that will be me"- if
u leave me- i will b there screaming - pushing a
shopping cart - begging the world to not hurt me -

and then there a too young girl who walks the
streets at night with only her shirt on screaming
at a family who long ago left- and then the scream
goes out to someone - the same one for hours- until it is night- will someone come for her- or will

people just walk by her – perpetuating the violent act of looking away

u see i come from the rivers of broken people where our eyes leak sorrow and our faces melt with pain - and the city sprays water on our bodies and calls us out our name- and we are less important than recycled bottles and only worth the price that our incarceration can get.-

Why did u leave me? Why did u leave and go away - taking my heart and throwing it goddam muth-fukinwhor street- u are a whore- anyway,slept with bush-iknowit i saw it- why did u leave and go away?

These women and men blend into the night sky becoming a shadow from a moonbeam – a doorway or just a memory in our mind

screaming out to the human race for eternally failing us to the lie of independence

and the violent act of looking away….

"el vaixells espanyols"

Paul Corman-Roberts
The Longest 12 Seconds

The 38 express
an ugly orange ramshackle
accordion segmented bus
I board most often around 6:10 AM,
a dragon rolling long
through the tapestry of Geary Street.

The driver, Missy, rarely shows interest
in putting on the brakes
all in the name of getting through that next light.
I'm never late for work
though I frequently experience neck pain.

One morning deep in the Tenderloin
the commuter packed next to me
a petite, elderly Asian woman
has the last turn at the exit.

Before she is able to get all the way out,
       one foot on the street,
the other on the back MUNI door's last step,
the hydraulics of the bus' back door
       snap around her ankle.

Missy needs to get to the next stop.
the woman's purse leaves behind
pens, applicators, cigarettes and change,
all bouncing and getting smaller behind her
the departing bus drags her flailing form.

We all scream "STOP!"
Missy yells "I don't stop for no goddamn
      late fare skippers!"

The longest 12 seconds later the bus comes to a stop
our commute ends with an ambulance ride
for a moaning but otherwise okay Chinese woman
and a transfer or walk for everyone else.

The chronicle reports Missy is on her
      second DMV suspension
Thanks to union's archaic appeals process,
I get one more ride with Missy later that week.

The following week, I am late to work
and sleep great for the first time in years.

Charlie Getter
Spanish boats

      didn't always have a
           crow's nest
   to look out from
        but someone
   always had to look out

so a someone
     a presumable spry someone
         had to climb the mast
     and stand atop the square rig

maybe they looped a rope
     around themselves
         in case they slipped

Spanish boats used to sail
     across a Spanish Ocean
         though no one thought it
was
         Spanish
       except for the
        Spanish

      and even then
         probably not all of them
      especially the
        Spanish
      who had to ride
        and guide those boats

Spanish boats used to
      try to
    stay together
      because the ocean
   was (is) big
      and the boats were not

Not every boat could keep up
    and sometimes
      standing atop the sail
    all you can see
      is the top of another sail
    and sometimes no sail at all

and you might wonder
>   did they founder
>   did they wander
>   did they remember
>   you were there?

as I stand on the mast
>   looking out at the vast
>   distance
>   and see your sail
>   dip below the horizon

>   is it your boat going down
>   or just away
>   or should I look
>   down
>   to see
>   if it's me
going under

Susan Kitazawa
School Nurse

Maneuvering
the cage-like grocery cart
through the aisles,
I notice
a thick discomfort
pressing from behind my breastbone.

It pushes on surrounding organs
pulling my attention away
from noble plans
for a family dinner
of fresh fish fillets,
nutrient-rich greens,
and whole grains.

Maybe
it isn't a solid mass
but something
hollow at center
more like an aneurysm
stretched thin
containing liquid
visceral sadness

the residue of days
spent among children
who live in rooms without food
since the grocery money
went for something else
that might dull a parent's pain.

Every day
there are the calls
from school to homes
where someone says,
Look
do you hear?
I don't care
if he's sick
if she's barfing
if he's got a fever
because he was fine
just this morning.
I don't care
if you think she passed out
because I know
she's faking.
I'm not coming in
to get him.
She can ride
the damned bus home.
Do you hear me?

I hear.

I hear
the fear
of words shot at you
from across the kitchen
demanding to know
who you're talking to.
You tell me double shift
janitorial job
rode the bus home at midnight.
I hear the baby's high-pitched crying
the talk show guests shrieking
while he demands again,
Bitch, who is that
on the phone?

Coughing
a wet
green phlegm cough
you tell him
it's OK.
You tell me
to tell your kid
to go back to class.

I hear your scarred-over pain
dressed to kill

and ready to fight the world
though you're still in
the blue janitorial uniform
you wore
collapsed on the couch
after sixteen hours at work.

Your kid sits here crying.

I don't cry
because I'm at work.

At home
I feed my own kid
canned chili over rice
instead of fresh fish fillets
and nutrient-rich greens.
Then we look for
a book on frogs
for a science report
and a light bulb
burns out in the living room
and a friend calls
to say her mom
died alone in her sleep
and I start another dark load
and do the paperwork
and make tomorrow's lunches.

Everyone is in bed for the night.

Then I cry
alone
and fall asleep
and dream
of funny little kids
noisily eating
sweet strawberry peaches
right off a tree
that looks just like
the one Grandma and Grandpa had

except that it's growing inside a house
with a whole lot of extra rooms
and a bunch of grown-ups
who look after each other
and all the children, too.

William Lautner
We ARE Different

We are the Hatfields and McCoys
Though more like the "Guns" vs the "Others"

The Guns are certain
    deadly certain
The Guns demand one view
    their view
The Guns have voices loud
    always loud
The Guns march aggressively
    overly aggressive, with sticks and stones
The Guns wear protective armor
    belligerent armor
The Guns use symbols
    "anti" symbols
The Guns seek death
    the death of rights, of individuals.

The Others are certain
    certain of the right to be, be free
The Others urge many views
    views inclusive, not exclusive
The Others have voices loud
    loud in unison, in camaraderie

The Others walk together
    together in masses, of many colors
The Others wear armor
    armor of compassion, of bruised skin,
        of ragged clothing
The Others use symbols
    symbols of caring, of yearning, of the abused
The Others seek peace
    the peace of the many, not the few.

These tribes have grown in their rhetoric
    in their distance.
These tribes have chosen leaders
    or leaders have chosen their tribes
        one, an egotistical narcissist
        one, a person of compassion
            who has dealt with tragedy, not caused it.

These are the tribes of the 21st century
grown stronger from warring 18th, 19th,
    20th centuries
grown into another civil war.
Who will survive?
Will we become LESS different?

Will there be any flowers left
    not for gravesites
    but for sights of joy, celebration?

Gregory Pond
the fillmore or less

the fillmore district's lore
lies behind a closed door
the latest attempt to
make jazz contemporary
and turn less into more
left a neighborhood displaced
the former "harlem of the west"
replaced by a temporary
that shifted to a more affluent
when higher rents were paid
by newcomers who had no clue
to the existence of the rich history
when the fillmore used to rule
and offered everything from
jazz to folk to rock to blues
with a slice of r&b, dash of country
and a plate of gospel too
all mixed with some
of the tastiest soul food
this side of the Mississippi
back in the day when they welcomed
black panthers and white hippies

before the promise of redevelopment
brought the area to its knees
leaving abandoned blocks
of once black-owned
restaurants, homes and shops
back in the day
when "the moe" was the place to be
and we were led to believe
black lives mattered more than they say
but any remnants of that age
have long since gone
all that's left are moments of recall
of way back in the day
when it was the destination
the place to go in san francisco
where blacks and blues used to rule
and the fillmore used to reign

Kim Shuck
San Francisco

Pick any street corner
Any
Bench any
Stoop
Any fourth star
In this city or over it
Sit quietly
You will hear the water of time
Keys rattling
Heart and innovation
Ramaytush wonderings
War and colonization and patience and the mint
        that only grows on the south side of
        that mountain right there
You will hear the poetry of place
Popcicle sticks scratching on the curb
Clap songs and
Jump rope spells and
Chess moves
Love curses
Every night in some back room QR Hand reads
        the future and the past in autopsied phrases
The Babar poems

Bob Kaufman's guerilla words shouted at the
    unsuspecting somewhere in North Beach
The skyline mutters poems that have been and
    poems to come
And if you stand in the Café La Boheme's door
    too long
You might hear Alfoncito yelling what we will
    choose to call a poem
Old Wives Tales still hover faint along Valencia
You can listen to the purring of the various fogs
As they pad over Eureka and Noe peaks
Wolo's paintings comment quietly on every new
    show in Kerouac alley
If your hearing is very good
Ambrose's dictionary runs on a loop
    in a certain bar
On a certain bar stool
And the faint laughter from Sam's jokes
    will still grind Brett's teeth
Prayers for the plague victims
In more languages than you can count
Mumble down Grant and twine with
    the poems of the Unbound Feet Three
There are songs of burying and unburying
    to be found all over the Richmond
Every corner
Every bench
Every headstone under the sand at Ocean Beach

Mary and Carol Lee and Paula
        talk story in classrooms at State,
        at tables in cafés turned to bars
John's words rattle justice
Through the rusting bars of Alcatraz and
        the voices of those taken in
        Captain Jack's War
have made them into their own songs too
More wealth in words
Than in all of the great libraries
        that have ever been

Contributors

Adrian Arias *(p15,40) "the ever brilliantly inventive visual poet of the gesturing Word,"* - Jack Hirschman, Emeritus Poet Laureate of San Francisco. His poetry was published in Peru, Spain, US and in Macedonia, where he won the prize for the best poem of the Festival, The Struga Poetry Evenings. Adrian uses his dreams as creative initiatives, which he makes come true in performances, community projects, paintings and poems.

Ruth Asawa *(p36)* was an American sculptor and educator. Her work is featured all over San Francisco as public art, and in museum collections worldwide. She was an arts education advocate and the driving force behind the creation of the San Francisco School of the Arts, which was later renamed in her honor. In 2020, the U.S. Postal service honored her work by producing a series of ten stamps that commemorate her well-known wire sculptures.

Mahnaz Badihian *(p59)* is a poet, painter, and translator. She writes In English and Farsi. She has published more than ten books of poetry and translation. Her latest poetry collection," Raven Of Isfahan" was published in 2019. An international anthology of Covid-19 poetry and art published in 2020. She has MA, DDS, and MFA in poetry. Currently, she is working on the novel" Gohar."

Lisbit Bailey *(p20)* is the Archivist at San Francisco Maritime National Historical Park and a member of the Revolutionary Poets Brigade. Her poem "Strength" is part of "Tarot in Pandemic and Revolution" forthcoming from Nomadic Press.

Jennifer Barone *(p13)* is the author of three books of poetry, her latest: *Saporoso, Poems of Italian Food & Love (Feather Press)*. She is the host of the *WordParty Poetry & Jazz Series,* a winner of the 2007 and 2012 SF Public Library's *Poets Eleven* contest for North Beach and has featured at *SF MoMa, DeYoung Museum, LitQuake, SFJazz,* and the *SF Public Library.* Visit: jenniferbarone.wordpress.com

MK Chavez *(p41)* is a Black Latinx writer and educator. She is the author of *Mothermorphosis, Dear Animal, (Nomadic Press),* and several chapbooks including, A Brief History of the Selfie (Alley Cat Books.) Her most recent work can be found in Academy of Poets Poem-A-Day series and at Golden Gate Park in San Francisco with the Voice of Trees projects.

Paul Corman-Roberts *(p63)* new collection of poems is *Bone Moon Palace* from Nomadic Press. He is the co-founder of Oakland's Beast Crawl Lit Festival, and hopes to regain a normal sleep pattern someday.

Since making San Francisco her home in 1977, **Kitty Costello** *(p17)* has worked at everything from apartment renovation to driving the bookmobile to being a psychotherapist and tai chi teacher. Poet friends who influenced her most include Diane di Prima, who taught her early on how to tap into the creative wellspring within, and Mary TallMountain, with whom she shared the delights and transformative power of writing in community. Her 2018 poetry collection is called *Upon Waking,* and she is co-editor of the 2021 anthology, *Muslim American Writers at Home: Stories, Essays & Poems of Identity, Diversity & Belonging,* helping to heal Islamophobia.

Tongo Eisen-Martin *(p21)* is an educator and organizer whose work centers on issues of mass incarceration, extrajudicial killings of Black people, and human rights. He has taught at detention centers around the country and at the Institute for Research in African-American Studies at Columbia University. He is the 8th Poet Laureate of San Francisco.

Anna Lisa Escobedo *(p28)* is a visual artist, muralist, artivist, event producer, cultural worker, and networker. Born and raised in Central Los Angeles, and since 2008 has been living in San Francisco. . She is a founder of Calle 24 Latino Cultural District and chaired the Cultural Arts Committee. Anna Lisa's goals are to pay artists and grow the vibrancy of the arts and culture ecosystem in the Bay Area.

Lourdes Figueroa *(p55)* was born in Yuba City, California during a trip her parents made from Mexico to the USA when they worked in the campo tilling the soil for tomatoes. Her work has been published in Something Worth Revising, Night Music, Spooky Actions Books published her first chapbook, yolotl, and her poem War America War was published by Backwords Press. She received her MFA in Creative Writing at the University of San Francisco. She is a native of limbo nation. Lourdes believes in your lung, your throat.

Charlie Getter *(P65)* was originally fashioned out of the mud of the west bank of the Vltava River in 1620, during the short reign of Frederick, King of Bohemia and Elector of the Palatinate (known to history as "the Winter King" for the duration of his prerogative.) He has been dissolved and reconstituted and re-vivified many times by various rabbinical scholars depending upon their need or inclination, his last iteration initiated on the eastern seaboard of North America sometime after the "Summer of

Love," after which, he seems to have been misplaced. He is rumored to be in San Francisco, but rumors are scarcely worth the air spent to breathe them...

Jack Hirschman *(p51)* was the fourth Poet Laureate of San Francisco. He was a poet and translator. Hirschman was the author of many books of poetry. He lived in North Beach

Nancy Hom *(p29)* has been an artist, writer, and curator in San Francisco for over 45 years. Through her posters, poetry, installations, and curatorial work, she has used the arts to affirm the histories, struggles, and contributions of communities of color. She has also nurtured the creative growth of over a dozen Bay Area arts organizations.

Clara Hsu *(p33)* is a San Francisco poet, playwright, actor and piano teacher. She caught a travel bug some years ago and it has been feeding her ever since. Clara received the Jefferson Award for public service in April 2021. She continues to bring poetry into the lives of people she touches.

Lauren Emiko Ito *(p27)* is a Gosei (fifth generation person of Japanese descent) poet, organizer, and curator whose art centers ancestral power, incarceration, and liberatory futures for generations to come. Her work has been published in anthologies, newspapers, and literary journals, including the *San Francisco Public Library*, *The City is Already Speaking*, *this is my body: an anthology of women of color reclaiming narratives of self and body*, *Endangered Species*, *Enduring Values*, and *sPARKLE & bLINK*. She has been featured by The Seattle Times, Japanese American National Museum, and The Beat Museum, and has received fellowships from the Asian American Women Artists Association, The Writers Grotto, among others.

Mason J. *(p14)* (they/them) is an Artist, Historiographer, and Community Organizer, influenced by life as a born and raised 2nd Gen. Nightlifer, Black and Native San Francisco Local, Jewish Mystic, Queer Two-Spirit, and Land Use advocate. They have worked with RADAR Productions, the James C. Hormel LGBTQIA Center, Transgender Cultural District. and GLBT Historical Society to ensure queer history is accurately documented. Mason's first chapbook, "Crossbones on My Life" debuted with Nomadic Press in Feb. 2021 and can be ordered @ nomadicpress.org/store/crossbonesonmylife

Randy James *(p26)* is California-born poet and educator. His work has been published in The Rumpus, Palette, and Red Cedar Review. His chapbook Shifters is currently available on Nomadic Press.

E.K. Keith *(p19)* usually plans for the worst, in hopes something else happens — like when you bring your umbrella and it doesn't rain. She is a Latinx poet whose work can be enjoyed in print, on the radio, online, and in person in the San Francisco Bay Area. Nomadic Press published her first collection of poetry, *Ordinary Villains*, in September 2018.

Tehmina Khan *(p23)* is a daughter of Indian immigrant scientists who has spent her adult life writing, teaching, resisting, and mothering. She has taught science to preschoolers and citizenship to octogenarians; she now teaches English at City College of San Francisco, where she defends everyone's right to a quality education.

Susan Kitazawa *(p68)* lives in San Francisco. She enjoys making art, writing, dancing, and community advocacy. She is retired after 25 years working as a registered nurse with low income and Immigrant people. She has university degrees in cultural anthropology, nursing, and education. She now lives with ever-decreasing eyesight but perhaps with ever-widening vision — her interest in the experiences of others and her own experience living life as an American woman of color, now with a deepening disability, are reflected in much of her creative work. Her writing has been published, with work forthcoming in the Fire Thieves anthology. She hopes that, by sharing her work, she can offer some light to others on this path that we all share.

William Lautner *(p73)* is an up and coming poet in the burgeoning platforms of the SF poetry scene. A stalwart member of the Bernal Heights Older Writers League, he has performed with the OWLS at Litcrawl and is scheduled to feature with the group again at this year's Litcrawl on October 23rd. He is currently working on his first collection of poems.

devorah major *(p53)* is an American writer, editor, recording artist, and professor. She has won awards in poetry, fiction, and creative non-fiction and is San Francisco's third Poet Laureate.

Norm Mattox *(p47)* is a retired educator whose poetry tells a story of love and resilience in these times of challenge, struggle, and transformation. Norm's first chapbook, Get Home Safe, Poems for Crossing the Community Grid, was published in 2016. Nomadic Press published his second chapbook, Black Calculus, released February 2021

Kathleen McClung's *(p11)* books include *Temporary Kin, The Typists Play Monopoly, Almost the Rowboat* and *A Juror Must Fold in on Herself*, winner of the 2020 Rattle Chapbook Prize. She teaches at Skyline College and serves as Guest Editor at *The MacGuffin*. www.kathleenmcclung.com

Florencia Milito *(p42,43)* is a poet, memoirist, and translator whose work has been influenced by her early experience fleeing Argentina's 1976 coup. Her bilingual collection *Ituzaingó: Exiles and Reveries / exilios y ensueños* was published in 2021 by Nomadic Press.

K.R. Morrison *(p45)* is a poet, drummer, and high school teacher from San Francisco. These days, she writes and teaches online by the sea, a place she calls Mermaidtown

Christine No *(p49)* [She/Her] is a child of Korean Immigrants. She is a Sundance Alum, VONA Fellow, two-time Pushcart Prize Nominee and Best of the Net Nominee. You can find her work in: The Rumpus, Entropy, Columbia Journal, The Harpoon Review, Story Magazine, sPARKLE+bLINK, Vagabond City, Apogee, Atlas And Alice, & various anthologies. Christine's first full length poetry collection is forthcoming by Barrelhouse. [Come say hi at: www.christineno.com / @iamchristineno]

Gregory Pond *(p75)* was born in Brooklyn to Panamanian parents, has written four books of poetry, is a member of Revolutionary Poets Brigade and facilitator of *Poetically Speaking,* a weekly conference-call program for seniors. He lives in San Francisco.

Dean Rader *(p35)* has authored or co-authored 11 books, including *Self-Portrait as Wikipedia Entry*. He is a professor at the University of San Francisco and the recipient of a 2019 Guggenheim Fellowship in Poetry.

Douglas A. Salin www.dougsalin.com, is known for his architectural lighting photography and publication mentoring. He is a noted word janitor. Kindly accept his humble apology for any words that have been bruised , misused or abused herein.

Karthik Sethuraman *(p39)* is an Indian-American living in California. His works have appeared in The Rumpus, AAWW, Fugue, and Fairy Tale Review, among others. His chapbook, Prayer under eyelids, is available from Nomadic Press.

Kim Shuck *(p44,77)* was the 7th Poet Laureate of San Francisco. Shuck has a bit more than a handful of solo books, the latest is Exile Heart from That Painted Horse Press.

James J. Siegel *(p37)* is a San Francisco-based **poet** and literary arts organizer. He is the host and curator of the popular monthly Literary Speakeasy show at Martuni's piano bar and author of The God of San Francisco.

As a young Lakota warrior who is currently struggling with houselessness in San Francisco , I find the theft of land today still appaling. My name is **Phillip Standing Bear** *(p58)* poverty skola to inform you of the atrocities of land theft. I can atest to the wrongful act of land theft through my own Lakota peoples Paha Sapa, or the Black Hills of South Dakota. Just like Oak Flats, the Black Hills was uprooted of First Nations Lakota peoples for the fact that gold resided in the depths of the land. Treaties were broken or never held, for the sake of profit. Even today treaties long been ignored are still uprooted for the sake of profits. The only way we get that land back is when it is destroyed and is no longer the place we once called home.

Sunnylyn Thibodeaux *(p25)* is a teacher, neighborhood activist and poet. She is the author of The World Exactly (Cuneiform Press, 2020), Universal Fall Precautions (Spuyten Duyvil, 2017), As Water Sounds (Bootstrap Press, 2014) and Palm to Pine (2011), as well as over a dozen small books including 88 Haiku, Against What Light, Room Service Calls, and What's Going On. Originally from New Orleans, she lives and writes in San Francisco and co-edits Auguste Press and Lew Gallery Editions.

Tiny *(p61)* poet, poverty skola formerly houseless/incarcerated visionary of Homefulness, teacher and Author of Criminal of Poverty Growing Up Homeless in America and co-author of How to Not Call PoLice Ever & Poverty Scholarship- Poor People Led Theory, Art, Words and Tears Across Mama Earth and the upcoming poetry collection The SideWalk Motel - Poems from a povertyskola & PoemOlogue Theatre Series- Sterile

Kimo Umu *(p46)*, formerly houseless youth skola, student at Deecolonize Academy and resident of Homefulness - a homeless peoples solution to homelessness.

Preeti Vangani *(p31)* is a poet, writer and educator. Her debut book of poems Mother Tongue Apologize (RLFPA Editions, 2019) was the winner of RL India Poetry Prize and her work has been published in Gulf Coast, Threepenny Review, Cortland Review among other journals. She works as a Poet mentor with Youth Speaks and holds an MFA (Writing) from the University of San Francisco.

Poet **Michael Warr** *(p34)* is a 2021 San Francisco Artist Grantee and 2020 Berkeley Lifetime Achievement Awardee. His books include *Of Poetry & Protest: From Emmett Till to Trayvon Martin* (W.W. Norton), *The Armageddon of Funk*, and *We Are All The Black Boy (Tia Chucha Press)*. His many awards include San Francisco Library Laureate, Creative Work Fund award for his multimedia project *Tracing Poetic Memory,* National Endowment for the Arts Fellowship, and a Gwendolyn Brooks Significant Illinois Poets Award.

Megan Wilson *(Cover Art)* is a visual artist, writer, curator, and community organizer based in San Francisco. Wilson has been an artist and core organizer with Clarion Alley Mural Project (CAMP) since 2001. In 2018 she co-directed and co-organized CAMP's second international exchange and residency project, Bangkit /Arise between artists from Yogyakarta, Indonesia and the San Francisco/Bay Area in collaboration with the Asian Art Museum of San Francisco. MeganWilson.com

www.ingramcontent.com/pod-product-compliance
Lightning Source LLC
Chambersburg PA
CBHW041927090426
42743CB00021B/3470